THE STENCIL COLLECTION
Nursery Design
Denise Westcott Taylor

Clowning Around   8

Out of the Toybox   12

Teddy Bears' Picnic   20

Safari Friends   24

Seaside Fun   16

Country Train   28

INTRODUCING STENCILLING

Once you begin stencilling you will be amazed at the wonderful results you can obtain quite easily and without spending a great deal of money. This book introduces six themed projects and provides ready-to-use stencils that can be used with numerous variations in design – just follow the step-by-step features and simple instructions. With very little paint and only a few pieces of equipment you can achieve stunning results. Have fun!

BASIC MATERIALS

Paints and Decorative Finishes
Emulsion paint
Water-based stencil paint
Oil sticks
Acrylic paints (bottles and tubes)
Specialist paints (for fabrics, ceramics, glass etc)
Spray paints
Metallic acrylic artists' colours (gold, silver etc)
Silver and gold art flow pens
Bronze powders (various metallics)
Gilt wax

Brushes and Applicators
Art brushes (variety of sizes)
Stencil brushes (small, medium and large)
Sponge applicators
Mini-roller and tray

Other Equipment
Set square
Blotting paper
Scissors or scalpel (or craft knife)
Roll of lining paper (for practising)
Eraser
Soft pencil
Fine-tip permanent pen
Chalk or Chalkline and powdered chalk
Long rigid ruler
Tape measure
Plumbline
Spirit level
Low-tack masking tape
Spray adhesive
Tracing paper
Paint dishes or palettes
Cloths
Kitchen roll
White spirit
Stencil plastic or card
Cotton buds
Methylated spirits

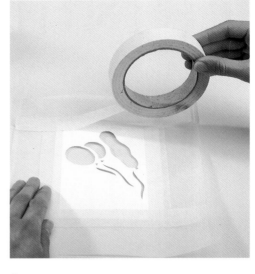

CUTTING OUT STENCILS
The stencils at the back of the book are all designed to use separately or together to create many different pattern combinations. Cut along the dotted lines of the individual stencils and make sure you transfer the reference code onto each one with a permanent pen. Carefully remove the cut-out pieces of the stencil. Apply 50 mm (2 in) strips of tracing paper around the edges using masking tape; this will help to prevent smudging paint onto your surface.

REPAIRING STENCILS
Stencils may become damaged and torn from mishandling, or if the cutouts have not been removed carefully, but they are easy to repair. Keeping the stencil perfectly flat, cover both sides of the tear with masking tape. Then carefully remove any excess tape with a scalpel.

GETTING STARTED

DUPLICATING STENCILS

Stencil plastic (Mylar) can be used; or card wiped over with linseed oil, which left to dry will harden and make the surface waterproof. Place the cut-out stencil on top. Trace around carefully with a permanent pen inside the cut-out shapes. Cut along the lines with a scalpel and remove the pieces. You may prefer to trace on top of the design, then transfer your tracing onto card.

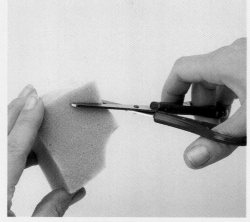

MAKING A SPONGE APPLICATOR

Sponging your stencil is one of the easiest methods, but you may prefer to use a stencil brush, especially for fine detail. Using a piece of upholstery foam or very dense bath sponge, cut pieces 12–50 mm (½–2 in) wide and approximately 50 mm (2 in) long. Hold the four corners together and secure with tape to form a pad. You can also round off the ends with scissors or a scalpel and trim to a smooth finish. The small-ended applicators can be used for tiny, intricate patterns.

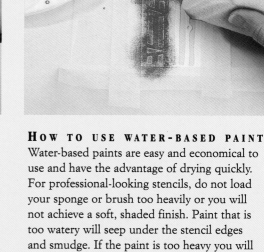

HOW TO USE WATER-BASED PAINT

Water-based paints are easy and economical to use and have the advantage of drying quickly. For professional-looking stencils, do not load your sponge or brush too heavily or you will not achieve a soft, shaded finish. Paint that is too watery will seep under the stencil edges and smudge. If the paint is too heavy you will obtain a heavy block effect rather than the soft stippling you require.

LOOKING AFTER STENCILS

Stencils have a long life if cared for correctly. Before cleaning make sure you remove any tape or tracing paper that has been added. Remove any excess paint before it dries, and wipe the stencil with a damp cloth every time you use it. If water or acrylic paint has dried and hardened, soften it with water and ease it off gently with a scalpel. Then use a small amount of methylated spirits on a cloth to remove the rest. An oil-based paint can simply be removed by wiping over the stencil with white spirit on a cloth. Stencils should be dried thoroughly before storing flat between sheets of greaseproof paper.

HOW TO USE OIL STICKS

Oil sticks may seem expensive, but in fact go a long way. They take longer to dry, allowing you to blend colours very effectively. Oil sticks are applied with a stencil brush and you need to have a different brush for each colour. Break the seal as instructed on the stick and rub a patch of the colour onto a palette, allowing space to blend colours. As the stencil sticks dry slowly, you need to lift the stencil off cleanly, and replace to continue the pattern.

PRACTISING PAINTING STENCILS

Roll out some lining paper onto a table and select the stencil you wish to practise with. Using spray adhesive, lightly spray the back of your stencil and place it into position on the paper. Prepare your paint on a palette. Dab your sponge or brush into the paint and offload excess paint onto scrap paper. Apply colour over the stencil in a light coat to create an even stippled effect. You can always stencil on a little more paint if a stronger effect is needed, but if you over apply it in the first place it is very difficult to remove. Keep separate sponges for different colours.

PLANNING YOUR DESIGN

Before starting to stencil take time to plan your design. Decide where you want to use the patterns, then work out how to position the stencils so that the design will fit around obstacles such as doorways and corners. The techniques shown here will help you to undertake the job with a systematic approach.

PUTTING PATTERN PIECES TOGETHER

1 Before you apply your design, stencil a sample onto lining paper. Mark the centre and baseline of the design on the paper and put together your pattern pieces. You can then work out the size of the design, how it will fit into the space available and the distance required between repeats.

2 You can avoid stencilling around a corner by working out the number of pattern repeats needed, and allowing extra space either between repeats or within the pattern. Creating vertical lines through the pattern will allow you to stretch it evenly.

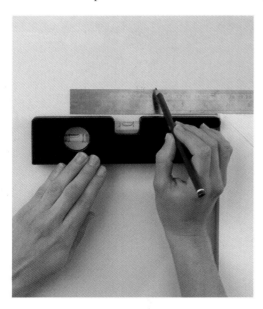

MARKING BASELINES AND HORIZONTAL LINES

Select your stencil area, and take a measure from the ceiling, doorframe, window or edging, bearing in mind the depth of your stencil. Using a spirit level, mark out a horizontal line. You can then extend this by using a chalkline or long ruler with chalk or soft pencil.

MARKING VERTICAL LINES

If you need to work out the vertical position for a stencil, hang a plumbline above the stencilling area and use a ruler to draw a vertical line with chalk or a soft pencil. You will need to use this method when creating an all-over wallpaper design.

FIXING THE STENCIL INTO PLACE

Lightly spray the back of the stencil with spray adhesive, then put it in position and smooth it down carefully. You can use low-tack masking tape if you prefer, but take care not to damage the surface to be stencilled; keep the whole stencil flat to prevent paint seeping underneath.

MARKING THE STENCIL FOR A PATTERN REPEAT

Attach a border of tracing paper to each edge of the stencil. Position the next pattern and overlap the tracing paper onto the previous design, tracing over the edge of it. By matching the tracing with the previous pattern as you work along you will be able to align and repeat the stencil at the same intervals.

COPING WITH CORNERS

Stencil around corners after you have finished the rest of the design, having measured to leave the correct space for the corner pattern before you do so. Then bend the stencil into the corner and mask off one side of it. Stencil the open side and allow the paint to dry, then mask off this half and stencil the other part to complete the design.

MASKING OFF PART OF A STENCIL

Use low-tack masking tape to mask out small or intricate areas of stencil. You can also use ordinary masking tape, but remove excess stickiness first by peeling it on and off your skin or a cloth once or twice. To block off inside shapes and large areas, cut out pieces of tracing paper to the appropriate size and fix them on top with spray adhesive.

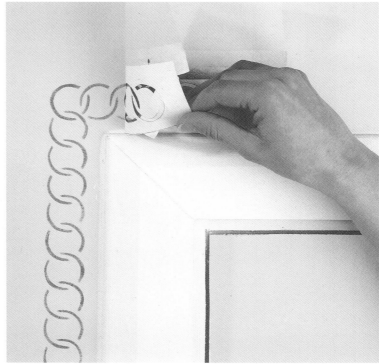

MITRING STENCIL PATTERNS

1 When you are stencilling a continuous pattern and need to make a corner, mask off the stencil by marking a 45-degree angle at both ends of the stencil with a permanent pen. Mask along this line with a piece of masking tape or tracing paper.

2 Make sure the baselines of the stencil on both sides of the corner are the same distance from the edge, and that they cross at the corner. Put the diagonal end of the stencil right into the corner and apply the paint. Turn the stencil sideways to align the other diagonal end of the stencil and turn the corner.

PAINT EFFECTS

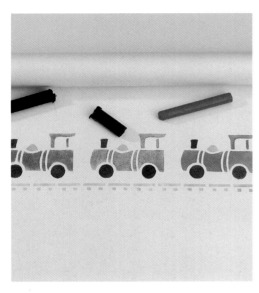

CHOOSING COLOURS

Take care to choose appropriate colours to create the effect you want. Stencil a practice piece onto paper and try a variation of colours to ensure you are pleased with the result. Different colours can make a design look entirely different. Use spray adhesive to fix your practice paper onto the surface on which you wish to produce the design so that you can assess its effect before applying the stencil.

APPLYING WATER-BASED COLOURS

Water-based paint dries quickly, so it tends to layer rather than blend. It is best applied by using a swirling movement or gently dabbing, depending on the finished effect you wish to create. Once you have applied a light base colour, you can add a darker edge for shading. Alternatively, leave some of the stencil bare and add a different tone to that area to obtain a shaded or highlighted appearance.

BLENDING OIL-STICK COLOURS

Oil sticks mix together smoothly and are perfect for blending colours. Place the colours separately on your palette and mix them with white to obtain a variety of tones or blend them together to create new colours. You can also blend by applying one coat into another with a stippling motion while stencilling. Blending looks most effective when applying a pale base coat, then shading on top with a darker colour.

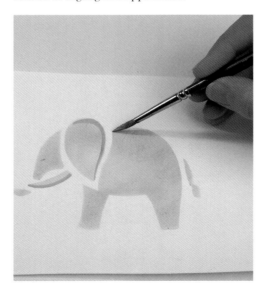

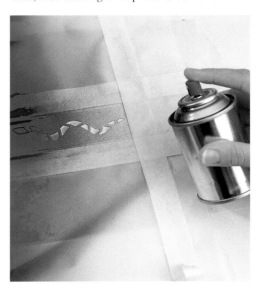

HIGHLIGHTING

A simple way to add highlighting to your design is first to paint in your stencil in a light tone of your main colour, then carefully lift the stencil and move it down a fraction. Then stencil in a darker shade; this leaves the highlighted areas around the top edges of the pattern.

GILDING

After painting your stencil use gold to highlight the edges. Load a fine art brush with gold acrylic paint and carefully outline the top edges of the pattern. Use one quick brush stroke for each pattern repeat, keeping in the same direction. Other methods are to blow bronze powder onto the wet paint, draw around the pattern with a gold flow pen, or smudge on gilt wax cream, then buff to a high sheen.

APPLYING SPRAY PAINTS

Spray paints are ideal on glass, wood, metal, plastic and ceramic surfaces. They are quick to apply and fast drying, but cannot be blended, although you can achieve subtle shaded effects. Apply the paint in several thin coats. Mask off a large area around the design to protect it from the spray, which tends to drift. Try to use sprays out of doors or in a well-ventilated area. Some spray paints are non-toxic, making them ideal for children's furniture.

DIFFERENT SURFACES

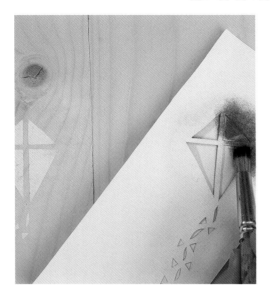

BARE WOOD

Rub the wood surface down to a smooth finish. Then fix the stencil in place and paint with a thin base coat of white, so that the stencil colours will stand out well when applied. Leave the stencil in place and allow to dry thoroughly, then apply your stencil colours in the normal way. When completely dry you can apply a coat of light wax or varnish to protect your stencil.

PAINTED WOOD

If you are painting wood or medium-density fibreboard (MDF) prior to stencilling, seal it with a coat of acrylic primer before adding a base coat of emulsion or acrylic paint. If the base coat is dark, stencil a thin coat of white paint on top. Apply your stencil and, if required, protect with a coat of clear varnish when it is completely dry.

FABRIC

Use special fabric paint for stencilling on fabric and follow the manufacturer's instructions carefully. Place card or blotting paper behind the fabric while working and keep the material taut. If you are painting a dark fabric, best results are achieved by stencilling first with white or a lighter shade. Heat seal the design following the manufacturer's instructions.

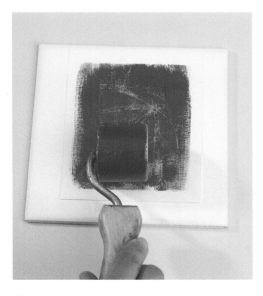

CERAMICS

Use special ceramic paints to work directly onto glazed ceramic tiles, and unglazed ceramics such as terracotta. Make sure all surfaces are clean, so that the stencils can be fixed easily. Apply the paint with a brush, sponge, spray or mini-roller. Ceramic paints are durable and washable, and full manufacturer's instructions are given on the container.

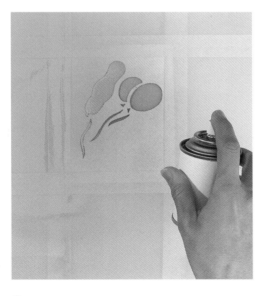

GLASS

Before applying the stencil make sure the glass is clean, spray on a light coat of adhesive and place the stencil in position. Spray on water-based or ceramic paint, remove the stencil and allow to dry. If you wish to stencil drinking glasses, use special non-toxic and water-resistant glass paints. An etched-glass look with stencils on windows, doors and mirrors can be achieved with a variety of materials.

PAINTED SURFACES

Stencils can be applied to surfaces painted with matt, satin or vinyl silk emulsion, oil scumble glazes, acrylic glazes and varnishes, and to matt wallpaper. If you wish to decorate a gloss surface, stencil first with an acrylic primer, leave to dry and then stencil the colours on top. Surfaces to be stencilled need to be smooth so that the stencil can lay flat.

PAINT COLOUR GUIDE

Bright red   Rose red   Rust red

Orange   Sunny yellow   Warm yellow

Turquoise   Silver (artists' acrylic paint)

Blue (interference paint)

PAINTING THE BIG TOP

1 Paint the walls with warm yellow emulsion and, when it is dry, mark evenly spaced vertical stripes.

2 Mix a glaze using rust red paint and an acrylic scumble. Apply it with a soft cloth in alternate stripes. Define the chevrons and the edges of the stripes with masking tape.

3 Repeat the clown (stencil B) as a vertical pattern in some stripes.

4 Use the clown (stencil F) combined with balls, stars and clubs (stencils C and E) to fill the remaining stripes.

CLOWNING AROUND

These happy clowns make a bright and jolly nursery decoration. They can be painted on walls, as here, or used to decorate children's furniture or bedding. I painted the walls to resemble a circus tent, with colourwashed stripes, and made the clowns balance, juggle and turn somersaults around the room. I used shades of red and orange, dotted with shiny blue spots and stars, turning this into a warm and cosy, but exciting, room.

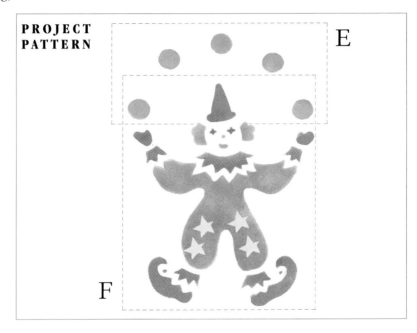

PROJECT PATTERN

E

F

POSITIONING THE CLOWNS
These clowns can be painted in variety of ways – upside down, juggling, balancing on one foot or holding up another clown. If your clown is juggling, paint him first, then position the balls, stars or clubs above his head to see which looks best.

PAINTING THE CLOWNS
Cut masks to keep areas of colour separate, such as the ruffs around the clown's neck, wrists and ankles. Apply the colour using a sponge. A coat of blue interference paint applied over other colours will give them a blue sheen.

ADDING STARS AND SPOTS
While the stencil for the clown is still in place, lay the star stencils over it. Paint through the stars so that there are half stars on the edges of his costume. The same method can be used to superimpose spots.

CLOWNING AROUND VARIATIONS

T he Clowning Around stencils can be combined in many ways and here are just a few to inspire you. Try painting the clowns as if they are turning cartwheels or have them balancing on a tightrope. Make each clown look different by varying the colours of his costume and the items he is juggling. Give him a club, a ball and an umbrella with which to struggle!

BALANCING CLOWNS (STENCILS A, D AND F)

STRONGMAN CLOWNS (STENCIL B)

ABOVE: JUGGLING CLUBS BORDER (STENCIL C)

LEFT: ROLLING BALLS (STENCIL E)

RIGHT: JUGGLING CLUBS ROUNDEL (STENCIL C)

RING PANEL (STENCIL D)

WAVY STAR BORDER (STENCIL E)

JUGGLING CLOWNS (STENCILS E AND F)

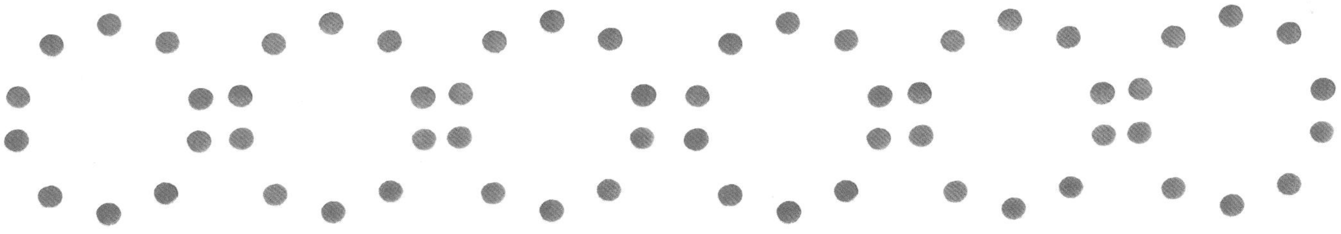

SPOT CIRCLES (STENCIL E)

UMBRELLA FRIEZE (STENCIL A)

**ROLLING BALLS
(STENCIL E)**

**RIGHT: RING CHAIN
(STENCIL D)**

PAINT COLOUR GUIDE

Red   Blue   Green

White

PAINTING THE HEADBOARD

1 Paint the headboard with two coats of white acrylic eggshell paint.

2 Mix a glaze using green paint and acrylic scumble. Brush the glaze onto the headboard and, while it is still wet, dab it with stockinette cloth to make a soft textured effect.

3 When the glaze is dry paint the rocking horses (stencil B) and the numbers (stencil A).

4 Finally, use a water-based varnish to protect your work.

OUT OF THE TOYBOX

Rag dolls and skipping ropes, toy drums and building bricks and, of course, a rocking horse – here are all the traditional nursery toys. I used the rocking horse to paint a child's bedhead in bright blues and greens highlighted with red. Change the colours to suit your own colour scheme. You could paint the designs on a toybox or shelf to encourage a child to put the real toys away at the end of the day.

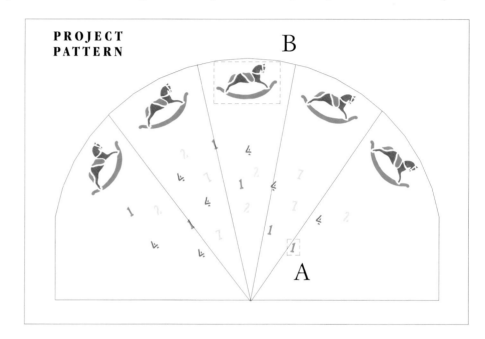

PROJECT PATTERN

B

A

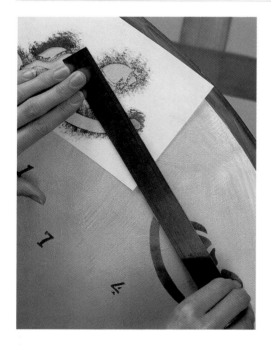

ARRANGING THE ROCKING HORSES
Measure the headboard carefully. Space the rocking horses to fit around the curve, starting at the centre. This headboard has just five evenly spaced horses. More or fewer horses can be used to fit larger or smaller beds.

ADDING NUMBERS
Paint the numbers in a random pattern below the rocking horses. The numbers are very quick to paint. Have several brushes ready so that you can paint them different colours. Combine numerals for numbers above ten.

PAINTING THE EDGE
This headboard has a bevelled edge and painting it with a colour gives it a pleasing finish. Using the green paint and an art brush, paint a stripe of colour. Steady your hand on the edge to avoid wobbling.

OUT OF THE TOYBOX VARIATIONS

Play with the stencils to find your own style, combining stencils and changing colours. The numbers can be combined with Toybox stencils or others in this book to make a counting frieze. Use the skittles and balls from the Clowning Around stencils, the kite from the Seaside Fun designs, elephants from the Safari Friends or sheep from the Country Train.

DRUM AND STICK BORDER (STENCIL E)

STACKING BRICKS (STENCIL C)

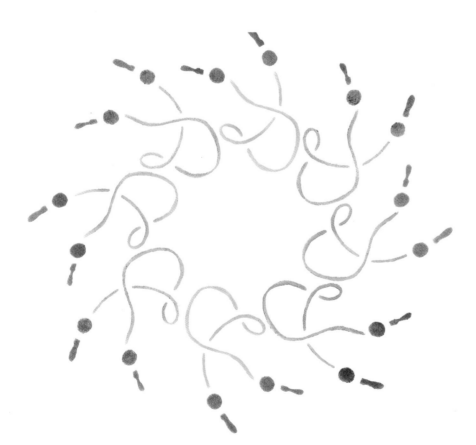

ONE TO TEN (STENCIL A)

DRUM STACK (STENCIL E)

SKIPPING ROPE CIRCLE (STENCIL D)

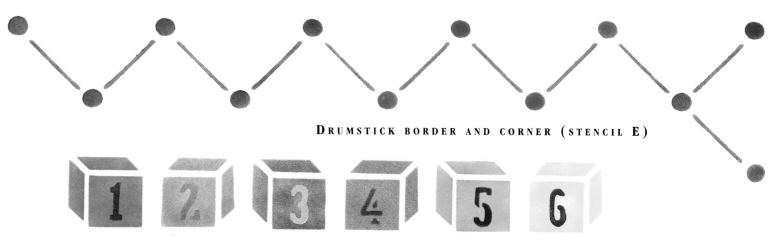

DRUMSTICK BORDER AND CORNER (STENCIL E)

COUNTING BRICKS (STENCILS A AND C)

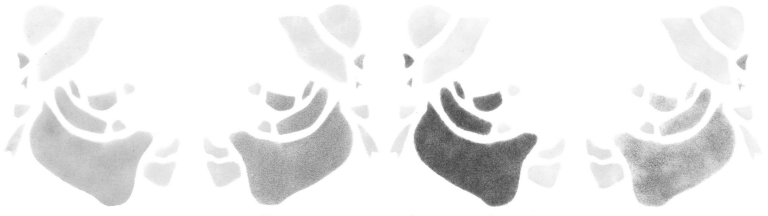

RAG DOLLS BORDER (STENCIL F)

SKIPPING ROPE BORDER (STENCIL D)

ROCKING HORSES BORDER (STENCIL B)

ONE ROCKING HORSE, TWO DRUMS, THREE BRICKS (STENCILS A, B, C AND E)

SEASIDE FUN

No more tears at bath time, the children's bathroom has been turned into the seaside! Paint the lower part of the walls in a sandy colour for the beach followed by a band of darker blue as the sea, topped by a clear blue sky. Then use the stencils to put in the details.

Look on other pages of this book for more ideas. Use the ball from Clowning Around as a beach ball or have a railway running through your scene.

PAINT COLOUR GUIDE

Sunshine yellow	Deep blue	Seà blue
Sky blue	Bright green	Bright red
White	Grey	

PAINTING THE SCENE

1 Paint the lower part of the wall sunshine yellow to represent the sand. I finished this yellow band just above the wash basin.

2 Use sea blue paint to paint the sea. Remember to make a straight, horizontal line for the horizon. Where the sea meets the sand the line can be wavy. Above the sea use sky blue to paint the walls.

3 Use all the stencils to make your seaside scene. The bucket and spade, being large, look better in the foreground, with the sandcastles and beach huts behind.

4 Varnish over the walls to protect your stencils and for ease of cleaning.

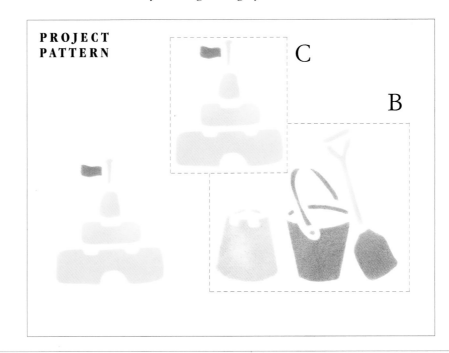

PROJECT PATTERN

C

B

ON THE BEACH
On the yellow background stencil all the things found on the beach. Mix a little red with the yellow paint for the sandcastles so they show against the sand. Paint white beach hut shapes before stencilling them in red, green and blue.

MAKING WAVES
Using stencil E, paint waves on the sea using dark blue paint, edging them with white if you want the sea to look choppy. Paint the boats bobbing about on the sea. Add extra seagulls in the sky.

THE SUN AND KITES
Paint the sun in a part of the room where it is naturally light. Fly the kites up in the sky and secure them by painting fine lines attached to a spade or the corner of a beach hut.

SEASIDE FUN VARIATIONS

BEACH HUT SQUARE (STENCIL F)

The seaside theme of these designs would be fun in an adult bathroom too. Use all or part of the stencils to create variations. The roof edge of the beach hut makes a bright zigzag border. The sun can be positioned over the sea so that it appears to be rising or setting, depending on your preference. Why not paint a floorcloth with a seaside theme for a bathmat?

DOUBLE KITES BORDER (STENCIL D)

SUNSET SCENE (STENCILS A AND E)

BEACH HUT ROOF FRIEZE (STENCIL F)

BUCKET AND SPADE-CIRCLE (STENCILS A AND B)

BEACH HUTS BORDER (STENCIL F)

UPSIDE-DOWN SANDCASTLES BORDER (STENCIL C)

SUNSHINE CORNER (STENCIL A)

FLYING KITES BORDER (STENCIL D)

SANDCASTLE BORDER (STENCIL C)

BUCKET AND SPADE FRIEZE (STENCIL B)

SAILING BOATS FRIEZE (STENCIL E)

TEDDY BEARS' PICNIC

Join the bear family for a celebration picnic on baby bear's birthday. Ribbons, bunting and balloons decorate their festivities and there is jelly and birthday cake for tea. All children love teddy bears and these, painted on the nursery chairs, will appeal to everyone. The birthday cake has separate candles and these can be added to the cake as your baby grows and used to practise counting skills. You could use some of the stencils to make birthday cards and invitations.

PAINT COLOUR GUIDE

Soft green acrylic eggshell

Sky blue acrylic eggshell   Dusty pink

Soft blue   Lemon yellow   Lilac

Mint green   Golden yellow   Terracotta

PAINTING THE CHAIR

1 If you are painting an old chair be sure it is in good condition, filling any holes and repairing loose joints.

2 Paint first with a primer followed with two coats of acrylic eggshell paint, green for the legs and seat and blue for the back. Sand between coats.

3 Use a combination of all the stencils to create the picnic scene.

4 Varnish the finished chair to protect it for many years of use.

PROJECT PATTERN

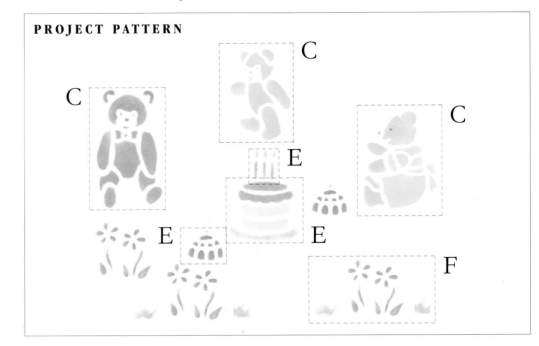

C   C   C   E   E   E   F

POSITIONING THE STENCILS
Arrange the teddies on the grass for a family picnic. Add extra family members by reversing the stencils and using different colours for the bears. The maypoles, bunting and balloons can be placed on the chair rails.

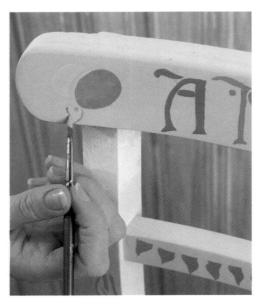

ADDING EXTRA DETAILS
Using an art brush paint a fine line up the chair back to represent the balloon string and stencil the balloons at the top. Using a sponge and a little white paint, add fluffy clouds. Dot the bears' eyes in with an art brush.

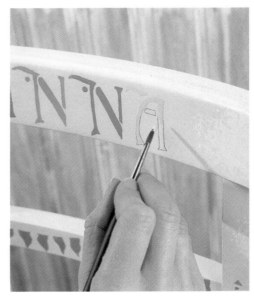

PAINTING A NAME
Find some lettering that you like and enlarge it to fit the chair rail. Transfer the outline of the letters onto the chair and use an art brush to fill them in with acrylic paint.

TEDDY BEARS' PICNIC VARIATIONS

Experiment with the Teddy Bears' Picnic designs to create your own scene. Use the stencils singly as in the flower rosette or combine them to make a picture. Look on other pages to find more stencils. The kite from the Seaside Fun stencils would look well in a picnic setting. Use strong primary colours for a bold alternative scheme.

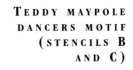

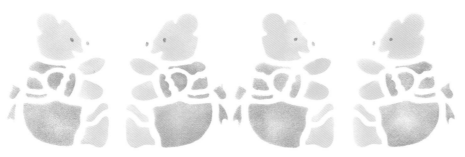

MUMMY BEARS BORDER (STENCIL C)

DADDY BEARS BORDER (STENCIL C)

BALLOON BORDER (STENCIL D)

BALLOON CIRCLE (STENCIL D)

FLOWER ROSETTE (STENCIL F)

TEDDY MAYPOLE DANCERS MOTIF (STENCILS B AND C)

BUNTING BORDER (STENCIL A)

WAVY BUNTING BORDER AND CORNER
(STENCIL A)

FLOWER FRIEZE (STENCIL F)

TEDDIES AND BALLOONS
BORDER (STENCILS C AND D)

JELLY AND CAKE BORDER
(STENCIL E)

MAYPOLE AND
BUNTING BORDER
(STENCILS A AND B)

WOBBLY JELLIES FRIEZE (STENCIL E)

SAFARI FRIENDS

So many wild animals – but these are all friendly! Use these animal designs to paint a frieze and as a fun way to learn all their names. I have placed the animals in a wide border around the wall, hiding behind the bushes and trees. Make them jump off the wall onto cushions, curtains or bed linen.

You could paint a Noah's Ark and line the animals up in pairs, queueing to board.

PAINT COLOUR GUIDE

| Olive green | Brown | Bright green |
| Green-yellow | Terracotta | Grey |

PAINTING THE WALLS

1 Paint the walls with two coats of green-yellow paint and the floor with bright green.

2 Stencil the walls with a random combination of animals, trees and bushes, flipping the stencils for more variety.

3 I enlarged the snake (stencil B) and painted it on the floor with red, using the balls from Clowning Around (stencil E) to paint its yellow spots.

4 Stencils on the floor need to be protected with several coats of varnish, especially in areas of hard wear.

PROJECT PATTERN

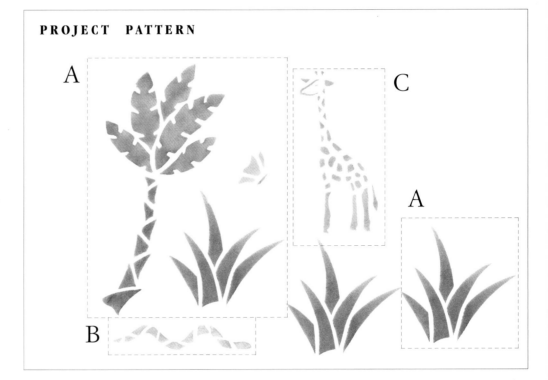

POSITIONING THE STENCILS
Holding the stencils to the wall, decide on the best positions for your animals and the vegetation. Place the stencils above each other to give an impression of depth. Some animals can be hiding behind plants.

PAINTING TREES AND BUSHES
Look at the variations (pages 26–27) to see how trees and bushes can be combined. The top of the palm tree can be used for a bush and extra leaves and fronds can be added by masking parts of the stencil.

PAINTING THE ANIMALS
Vary the intensity of paint to give more texture to the animals. Place an animal stencil so it overlaps a bush, then paint the animal stencil, taking care not to paint over the bush – the animal will seem to be hiding.

SAFARI FRIENDS VARIATIONS

The Safari Friends designs can be painted singly or put together to make a complete scene. Make a train of elephants holding tails or an abstract pattern of snakes. Use unrealistic colours to create a fantasy effect. Paint the animals around the edge of a nursery table to make teatime fun, or on a toybox. Or use fabric paint to decorate table linen for a party.

ABOVE: BUTTERFLY CIRCLE (STENCIL A)

WRIGGLY SNAKES BLOCK (STENCIL B)

RIGHT: VERTICAL GIRAFFE BORDER (STENCIL C)

TREES AND BUSHES BORDER (STENCIL A)

WRIGGLY SNAKES BORDER (STENCIL B)

ELEPHANT TRAIN (STENCIL E)

BUTTERFLY BORDER (STENCIL A)

TIGER LINE (STENCIL D)

DESERT PLANTS BORDER (STENCIL A)

HORIZONTAL GIRAFFE BORDER (STENCIL C)

COUNTRY TRAIN

PAINT COLOUR GUIDE

Grass green	Deep blue	Leaf green
Scarlet	Yellow	Brown
Black	Grey	

PAINTING A WALLPAPER DESIGN

1 Use artists' canvas for the floorcloth. Buy enough canvas to turn a hem on each edge.

2 The floorcloth is prepared by painting the canvas with emulsion paint.

3 Paint a circular railway track (stencil E). In each corner of the mat I painted a tree (stencil A), some fencing (stencil D), a train (stencil E) and sheep (stencil C). You could use this layout or create your own scene.

4 After stencilling, fold the turnings to the back, trim the corners and glue the hem in place on the cloth.

5 Finish with several coats of varnish.

6 Roll, but never fold, the finished floorcloth.

T hese little trains go puffing through the country, passing trees, fields and fluffy sheep, carrying goods and stopping at signals – a delightful and timeless scene with lots of interest.

Reviving a traditional craft, I painted a canvas floorcloth to use as a play mat. It can provide many hours of play while stimulating a young child's imagination and can be made to any size, is durable and easy to clean.

Why not paint a floorcloth as an unusual present for a new baby?

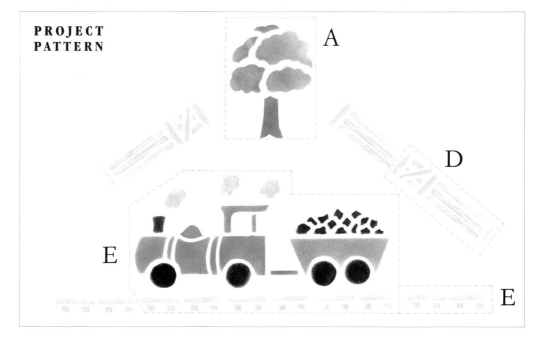

PROJECT PATTERN

A

D

E

E

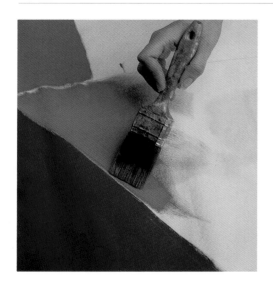

PAINTING THE CANVAS
Stretch the canvas out on a flat surface and, using grass green, yellow and red paints, cover the surface so that it resembles fields. Put on at least two coats, letting each dry thoroughly. Use a fine grade sandpaper to rub down between the coats of paint.

PLANNING THE SCENE
Paint the designs onto paper, cut them out and use these to plan the layout. When you are happy with the scene mark the positions of the stencils with a soft pencil or masking tape and begin painting.

FILLING THE TRUCKS
It is fun to 'fill' the empty trucks with logs or sheep. Paint the truck first, then place a tree stencil so it is partly overlapping the truck. Paint the trunk being careful not to paint over the truck.

COUNTRY TRAIN VARIATIONS

Vary the appearance of the train by changing colours and adding extra trucks. You could have one long train running right around a room. Omit the tree trunks and you have bushes or hedges. The sheep look lovely as a border and it would be fun to paint them in pastel colours for a young baby. Use parts of the track and signal stencils to make abstract patterns.

SIGNALS ROSETTE (STENCIL B)

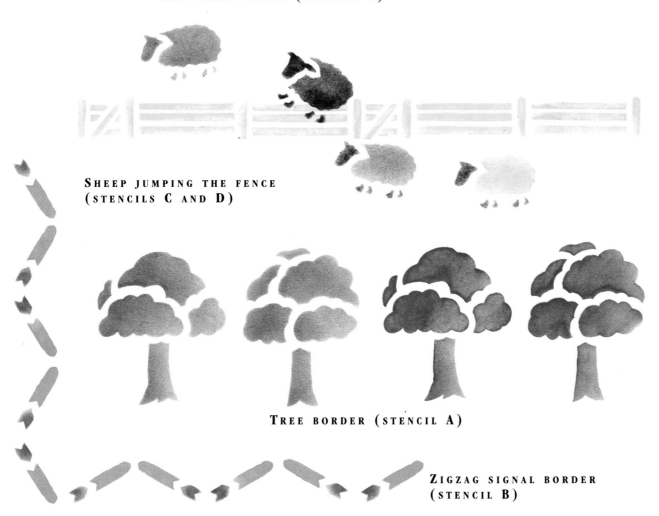

RED TRAIN MOTIF (STENCIL E)

SHEEP JUMPING THE FENCE (STENCILS C AND D)

TREE BORDER (STENCIL A)

ZIGZAG SIGNAL BORDER (STENCIL B)

DOUBLE SIGNAL EDGING (STENCIL B)

TRACK SQUARES BORDER (STENCIL E)

SIMPLE FENCE (STENCIL D)

SHEEP BORDER (STENCIL C)

SIMPLE SIGNAL EDGING (STENCIL B)

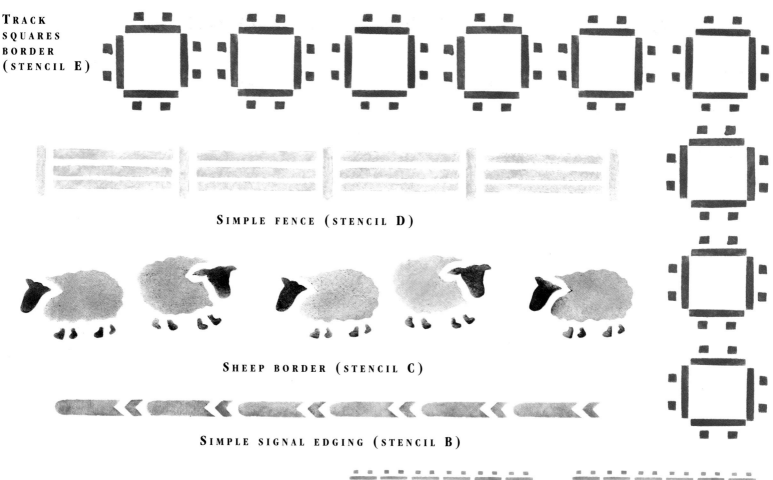

SIGNALS BORDER (STENCIL B)

BLUE ENGINE AND TRACK FRAME (STENCIL E)

GREEN GOODS TRAIN PICTURE (STENCILS A, C AND E)

SUPPLIERS

Emulsion paints are easily obtainable from DIY stores and good hardware stores; contact manufacturers below for your nearest supplier. Oil sticks and acrylic paints can be obtained from artists' materials stores. Other stencilling supplies can usually be found in any of the above and there are many dedicated stencil stores.

Imperial Chemical
Industries plc (ICI)
(Dulux paints)
Wexham Road
Slough
SL2 5DS
(Tel. 01753 550000)

Crown Decorative
Products
PO Box 37
Crown House
Hollins Road
Darwen
Lancashire
(Tel. 01254 704951)

Fired Earth plc
Twyford Mill
Oxford Road
Adderbury
Oxfordshire
(Tel. 01295 812088)

ACKNOWLEDGEMENTS

Thanks to Christopher, Guy and Gregory Taylor for their support and encouragement and to Karen, Graeme, Clare and Colin for their enthusiasm.

Merehurst wish to thank the following for their help:
Hamleys of London; Till Joinery, Banstead; Traditional Toys, London.

First published in 1998 by Merehurst Limited
Ferry House, 51–57 Lacy Road, Putney, London SW15 1PR

© Copyright 1998 Merehurst Limited

ISBN 1-85391-607-2

A catalogue record of this book is available from the British Library.

Edited by Geraldine Christy
Photography by Graeme Ainscough
Styling by Clare Louise Hunt

Colour separation by Bright Arts (HK) Limited
Printed in Singapore

Denise Westcott Taylor teaches stencilling and paint effects courses as well as taking on private commisions. She is also currently teaching a City and Guilds course on working designs for creative studies.